Fish Tale #1: Sammy Spinner

SUSAN DUKE

Illustrated by: Jose Tecson

To order additional copies of this book, contact:
Xlibris
844-714-8691
www.Xlibris.com
Orders@Xlibris.com

ISBN: Softcover   978-1-6698-2354-4
        Hardcover   978-1-6698-2355-1
        EBook   978-1-6698-2353-7

Library of Congress Control Number: 2022908351

Print information available on the last page

Rev. date: 05/04/2022

For all young fishermen who spend time on the water
hoping the next strike on the line is the biggest catch of the day,
may you have many fun-filled days of successful fishing
and learn the importance of catch and release along the way!

To my wonderful husband, Adam, who has taught me everything about fishing and still helps me to take fish off the hook, thank you! Your encouragement, guidance, and overall awesomeness for others learning how to fish, and finding the right spot in a lake to catch fish, are things for which you have exceptional talent. Thank you for your encouragement and support with this project, and for creating amazing adventures for us and our dogs on lakes in the Northwoods!

The gentle rocking of the red boat, along with the roaring start of the motor, woke the fishing lures in the tackle box from their off-season slumber.

Each fishing lure—those brightly colored and nearly perfect and those with dull or chipped paint and slightly tarnished hooks—began to rattle with excitement. They could hardly wait for their fishing adventure to begin.

These lures traveled through the Northwoods lakes, having fun as they were tossed in and dragged out of the water every summer. Each fishing lure moved through the water in different ways, but they each dived in with the same goal ...

to catch the fish!

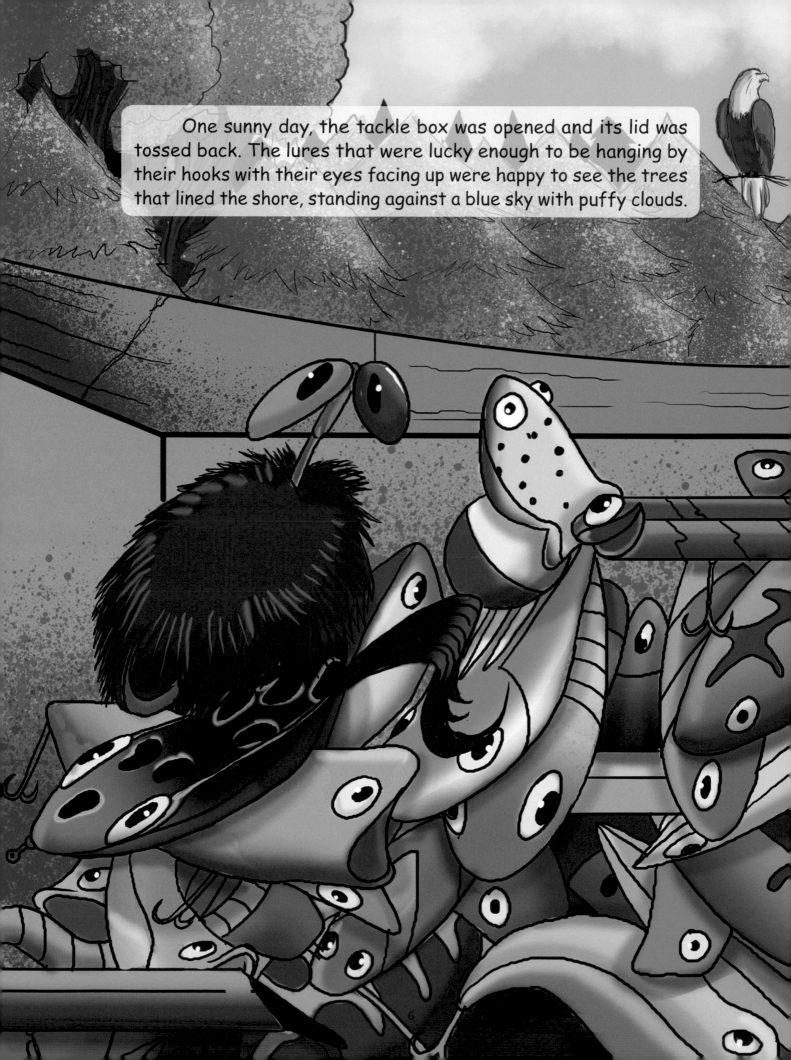

One sunny day, the tackle box was opened and its lid was tossed back. The lures that were lucky enough to be hanging by their hooks with their eyes facing up were happy to see the trees that lined the shore, standing against a blue sky with puffy clouds.

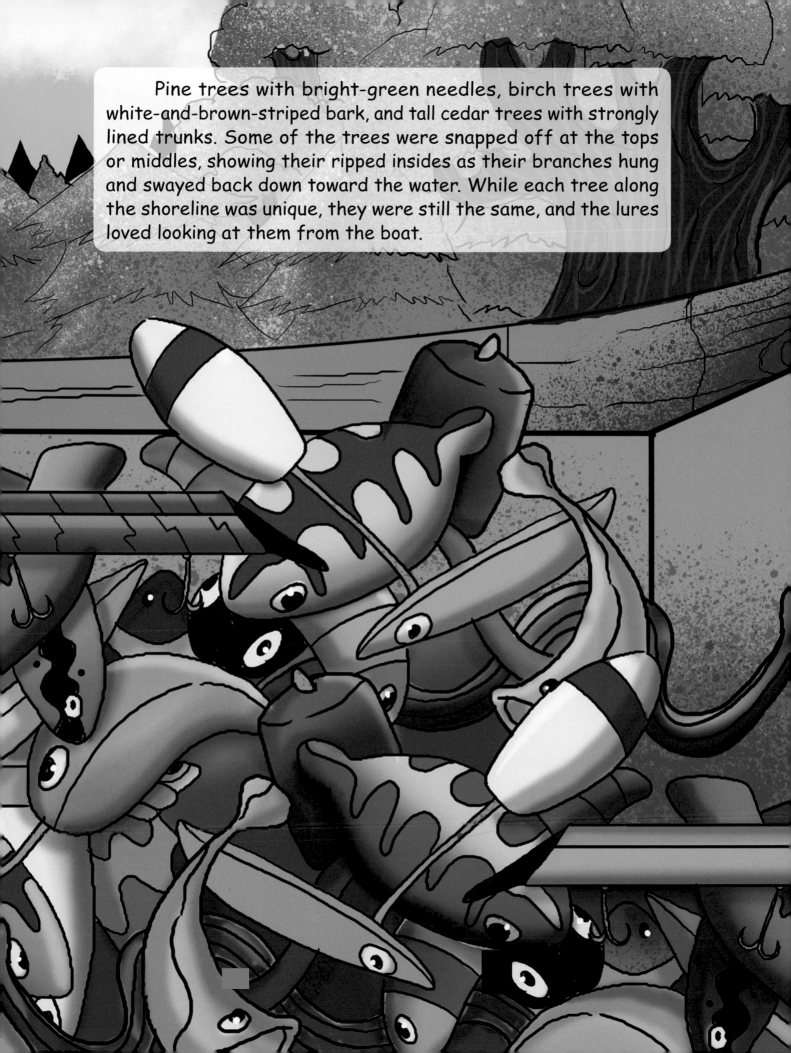

Pine trees with bright-green needles, birch trees with white-and-brown-striped bark, and tall cedar trees with strongly lined trunks. Some of the trees were snapped off at the tops or middles, showing their ripped insides as their branches hung and swayed back down toward the water. While each tree along the shoreline was unique, they were still the same, and the lures loved looking at them from the boat.

The fishing lures that did not have the beautiful view of the Northwoods enjoyed hearing the sounds of nature around them. The echoing calls from black-and-white loons as they swam across the water. The high-pitched giggles of bald eagles sitting in their huge, woody nests. The beaver's thick tail slapping mud in the openings of his dam, and the lake water popping as the bass were snatching insects from the surface.

8

"Listen, Bucky," replied a sneaky suick named Suki. "We hope you have learned how to shake the weeds loose and dry off when you are done fishing so that you don't stink when you come back into our box."

The other fishing lures shook by their hooks as they chuckled at Suki's slight dig at Bucky. It was true. Bucky had an awful smell he could not seem to shake, but he was nearly perfect in every other way. He was so good at fishing that the man in the boat called him a "great lure that does the job well."

The fishing lures in the box were so focused on the chatter between these two baits that they didn't notice a new lure as it was plopped down into the tackle box.

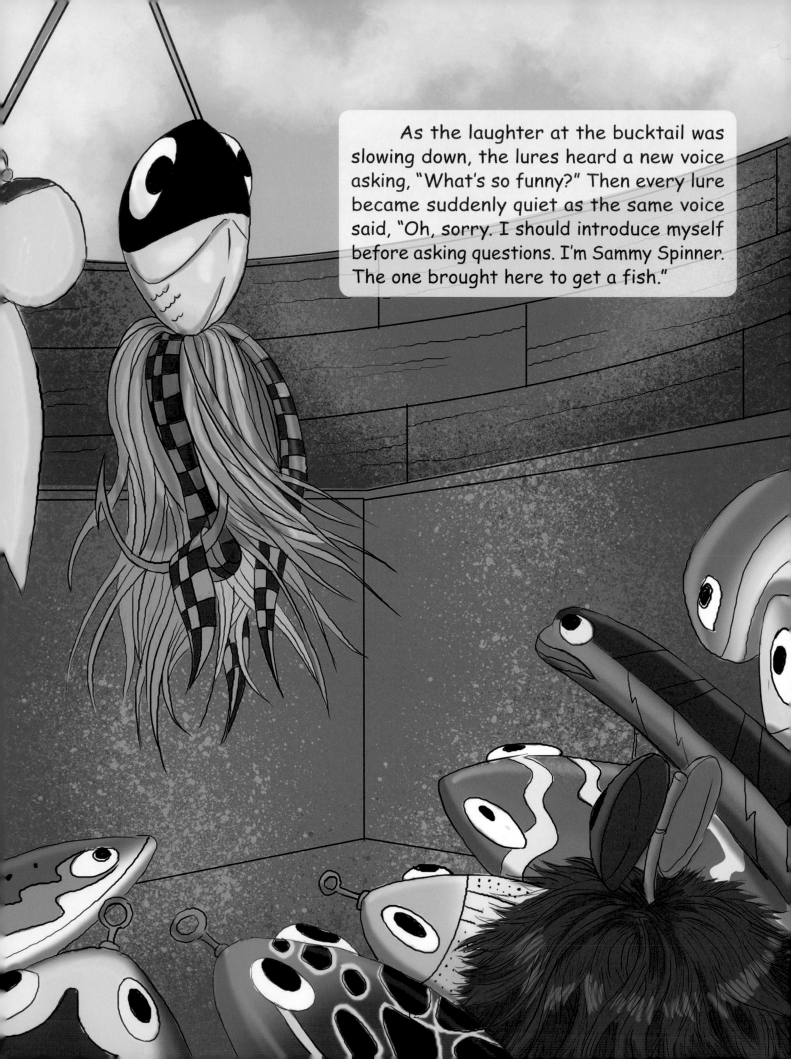

As the laughter at the bucktail was slowing down, the lures heard a new voice asking, "What's so funny?" Then every lure became suddenly quiet as the same voice said, "Oh, sorry. I should introduce myself before asking questions. I'm Sammy Spinner. The one brought here to get a fish."

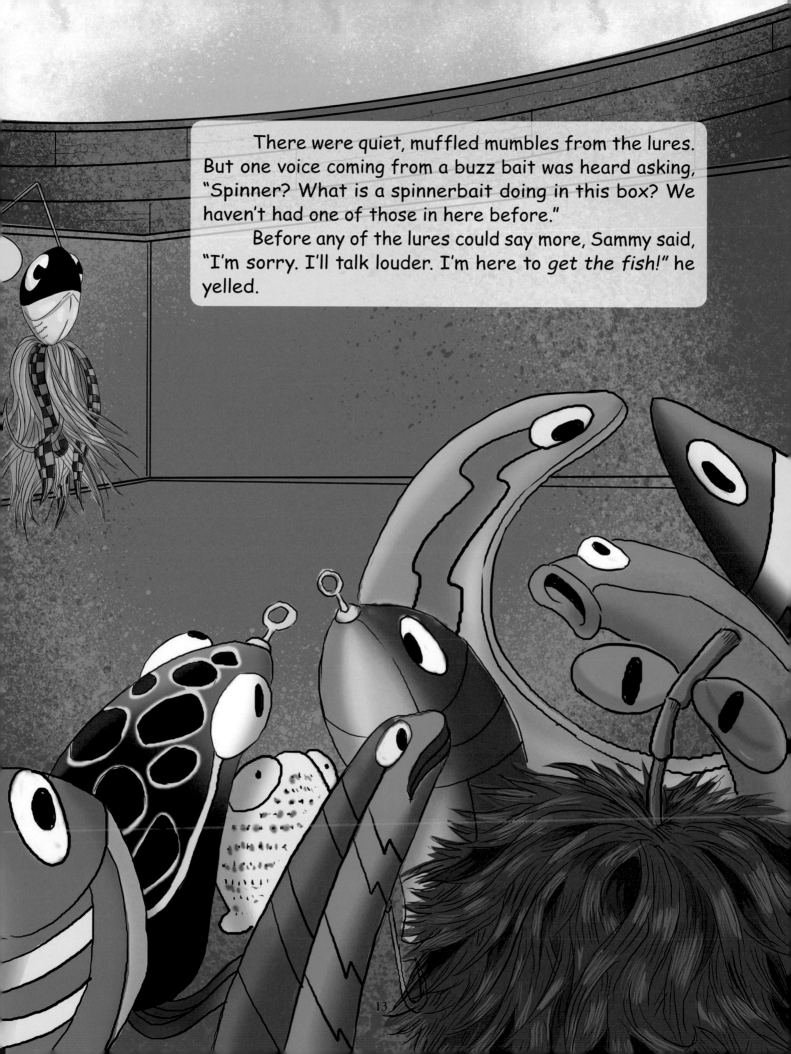

There were quiet, muffled mumbles from the lures. But one voice coming from a buzz bait was heard asking, "Spinner? What is a spinnerbait doing in this box? We haven't had one of those in here before."

Before any of the lures could say more, Sammy said, "I'm sorry. I'll talk louder. I'm here to *get the fish!*" he yelled.

13

Some of the lures rolled their eyes in response as Suki Suick said,
"Here we go again, a newbie with no real idea of what it takes out here."

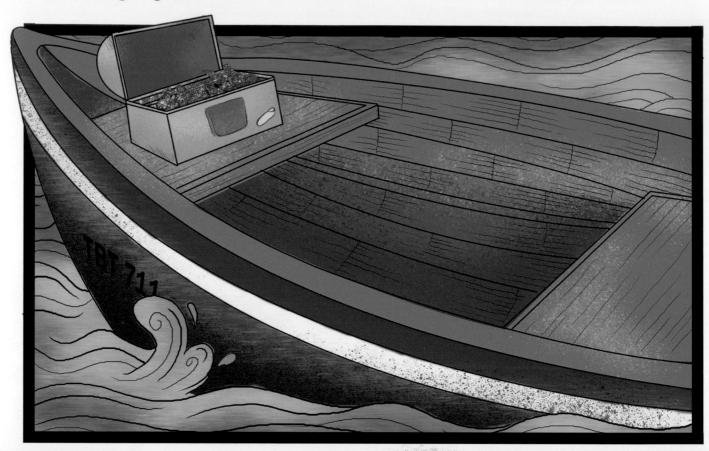

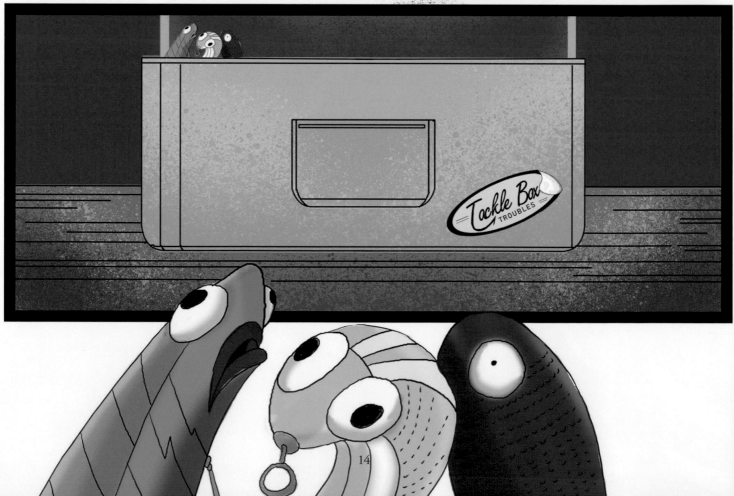

Sammy was shocked. "What do you mean? I'm not a newbie! I had to pass tests before being packaged, purchased, and brought here to get the fish. I was hooked up to a rod, dropped in a big fish tank, and moved back and forth until I snatched up a fish. I did it. I know my job. I'm ready!"

"Listen, kid. I hear you. Each of us has a similar story," Bucky said. "But until you've been thrown through chilly Northwoods air and hit the dark, murky water, gotten dragged through slimy weeds, or banged into hard edges of huge rocks scarred with propeller gashes—"

"Or wrapped up in a lily pad and sucked underneath the water unexpectedly," jumped in Francis, a rubber frog.

"You don't know the job. You're not ready," Bucky Bucktail finished. Then, while looking over at Francis Frog, Bucky said, "I notice you didn't learn during the off-season to stop jumping in and croaking out your thoughts while others are speaking."

Sammy replied, "I'm ready, but if you think I can learn more on how to get fish from the lures in this box, then—"

"We all have the same goal," Bucky interrupted.

"To *catch the fish!*" each lure in the box shouted at the same time.

"That's right. We don't get fish; we catch them. It's called fishing," continued Bucky.

Sammy replied, "I can see the frog isn't the only one needing to work on not jumping in when someone is speaking." The lures were surprised at how Sammy was talking to Bucky. Bucky Bucktail had been in the tackle box the longest and knew all there was to know about catching the fish.

Just then, a man's voice could be heard from above. "The water here is about nine feet deep with weeds two to three feet off the bottom. It's an excellent spot to try out your new spinnerbait."

As Sammy was plucked out of the box, he looked back and yelled, "I told you I was brought here for this! And the man in the boat thinks I'm ready too!"

He was attached to a line on a rod and dangled above the lake. As Sammy Spinner was being cast over the water, the other lures in the boat watched and listened.

Sammy was elated to be flying high above the water. His enthusiasm led him to flip and flop sideways and backward like a gymnast. When he hit the water, his body was sideways and not prepared to swim. He sank quickly and was suddenly yanked downward, becoming stuck in long, grassy weeds. Sammy freed himself and was pulled up through the water.

While skimming across the top of the water, back toward the red boat, Sammy thought his first dive in the lake didn't go as well as his dive tests. He had never landed on his side or seen such dark water in the lure-making factory. If Sammy was ever going to catch a fish, he would have to try harder next time.

Sammy heard the other lures talking as he swung back and forth on the line preparing for his second cast.

"Ha, ha, ha! Did you see his landing?"

"No, but I heard the splash. It could not have been pretty."

"Give him a chance" was the last thing Sammy heard Suki say as he was tossed out over the water again.

22

Sammy focused on his landing as a vibrant blue dragonfly whizzed by his head. This time his landing was perfect, but he was shocked by the cold, dark water that ran by his yellow and red blades as they went spinning in the water. Sammy could barely see as he was quickly pulled through long seaweed that tried to grab his hooks.

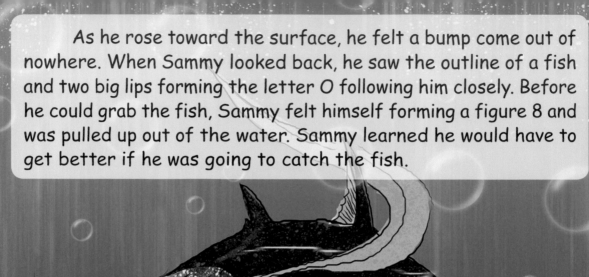

As he rose toward the surface, he felt a bump come out of nowhere. When Sammy looked back, he saw the outline of a fish and two big lips forming the letter O following him closely. Before he could grab the fish, Sammy felt himself forming a figure 8 and was pulled up out of the water. Sammy learned he would have to get better if he was going to catch the fish.

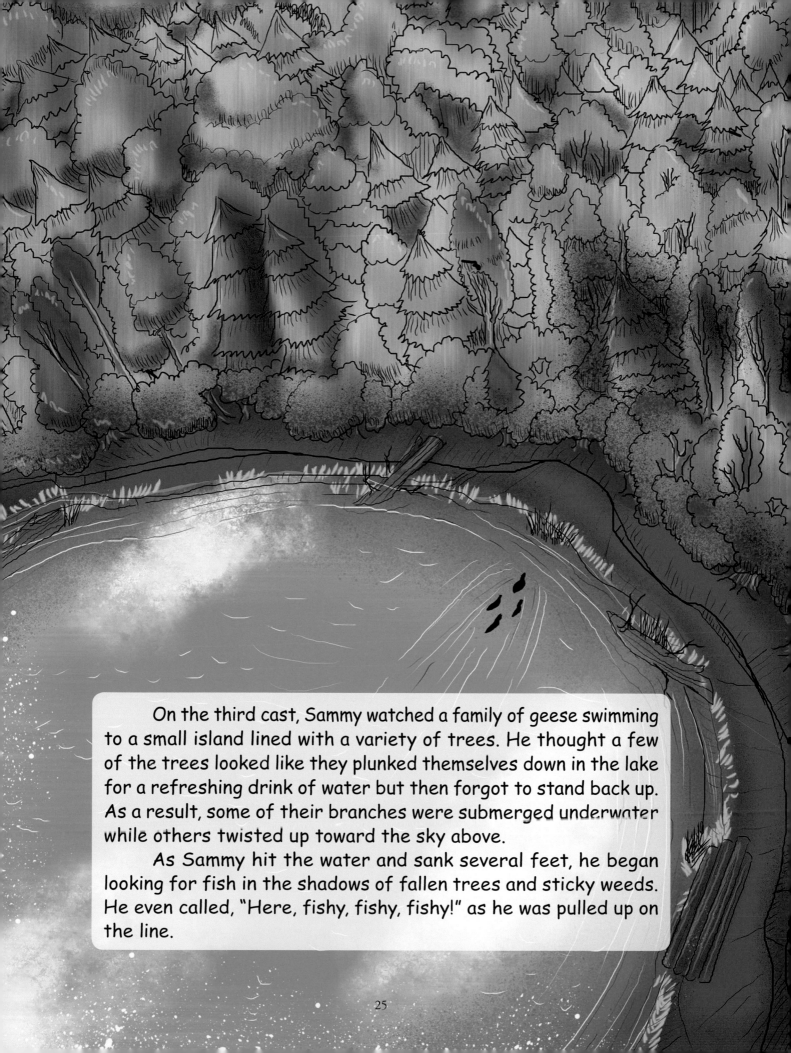

On the third cast, Sammy watched a family of geese swimming to a small island lined with a variety of trees. He thought a few of the trees looked like they plunked themselves down in the lake for a refreshing drink of water but then forgot to stand back up. As a result, some of their branches were submerged underwater while others twisted up toward the sky above.

As Sammy hit the water and sank several feet, he began looking for fish in the shadows of fallen trees and sticky weeds. He even called, "Here, fishy, fishy, fishy!" as he was pulled up on the line.

Sammy finally felt a nibble on his tail. He tried to grab the fish with his hooks, but it quickly swam away as another loud splash landed nearby. When Sammy came out of the water, he saw the bucktail swinging from the rod next to him.

Bucky smiled and said, "Sorry to ruin your first catch with my big splash. Let me teach you a quick lesson. Fish get spooked easily, so be quiet and work quickly while you are fishing."

As Sammy tried and tried again, he learned Bucky Bucktail was right; he needed to get more practice. So each day, Sammy learned fishing tips from the other lures as he hung in the tackle box, swung from different rods, or sat on the carpeted, thin ledge in the boat while drying off.

Sammy learned from a lure named Musky Ike to go slow and low on sunny days when the water was clear. From a topwater lure called Buzz Bait, he learned to go faster in the water to stay higher over the weeds. The spinnerbait learned to avoid snagging himself on piers, logs, and rocks from a watermelon-colored wacky worm. Sammy also had a lesson on how to keep his blades spinning during a perfect figure 8.

The tackle box of lures worked together every day to teach Sammy tips on being the best lure he could be. He made mistakes along the way but pushed himself to be better. Even Bucky Bucktail noticed Sammy Spinner becoming a smarter fish bait.

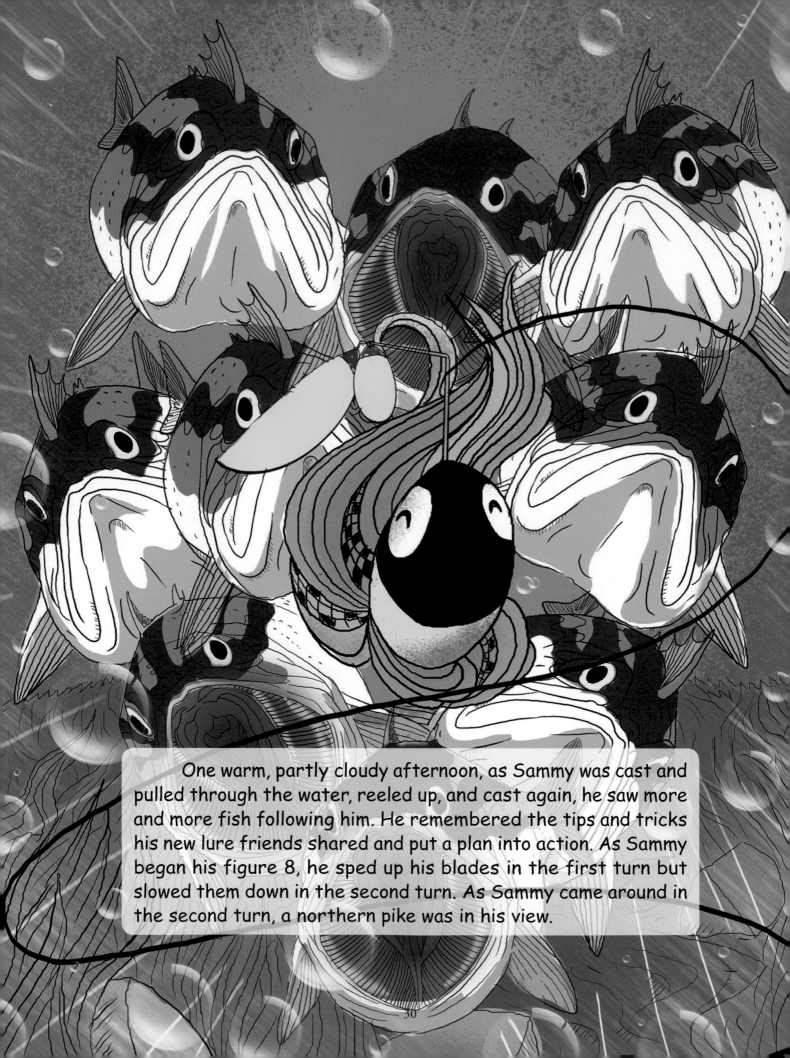

One warm, partly cloudy afternoon, as Sammy was cast and pulled through the water, reeled up, and cast again, he saw more and more fish following him. He remembered the tips and tricks his new lure friends shared and put a plan into action. As Sammy began his figure 8, he sped up his blades in the first turn but slowed them down in the second turn. As Sammy came around in the second turn, a northern pike was in his view.

The northern pike gulped Sammy into its mouth, and Sammy stuck his hooks in. It twisted and flipped Sammy in all different directions. Sammy almost let go. But then he remembered he needed to work with the rod to reel himself and the fish up to the boat.

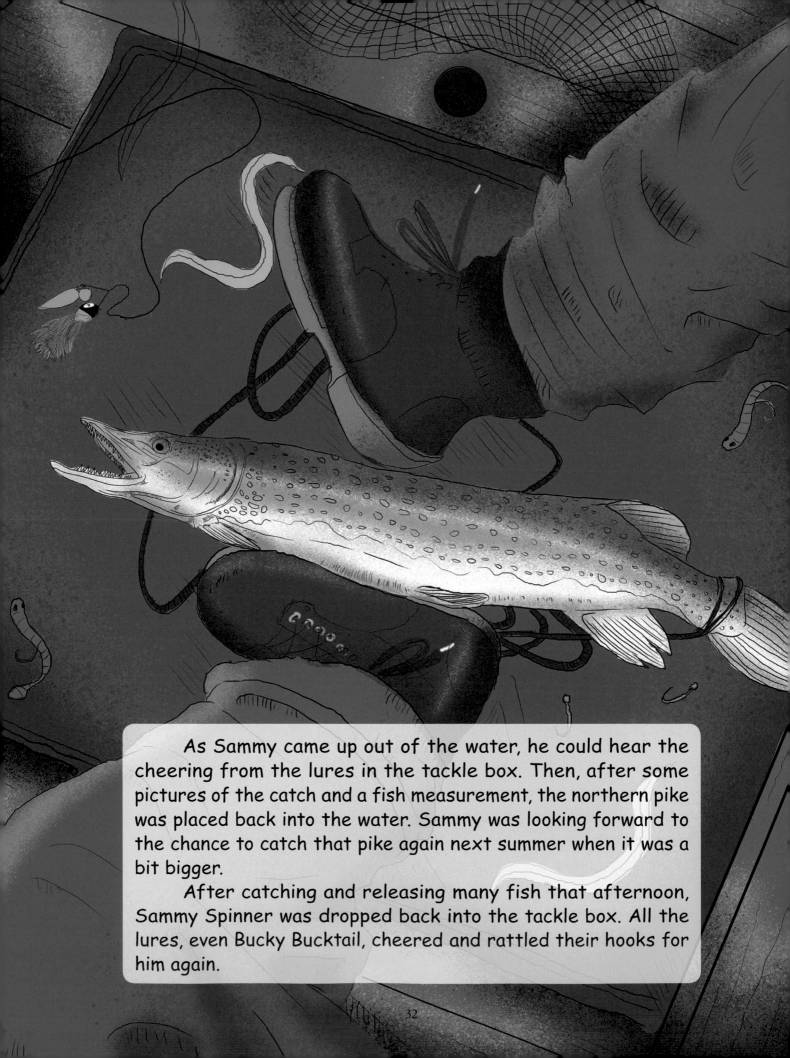

As Sammy came up out of the water, he could hear the cheering from the lures in the tackle box. Then, after some pictures of the catch and a fish measurement, the northern pike was placed back into the water. Sammy was looking forward to the chance to catch that pike again next summer when it was a bit bigger.

After catching and releasing many fish that afternoon, Sammy Spinner was dropped back into the tackle box. All the lures, even Bucky Bucktail, cheered and rattled their hooks for him again.

Sammy's paint was chipped, a spinner came unattached, and his metal frame was slightly bent from the fish tugging on him, but he was proud of his catch. "I can't believe how difficult fishing can be!" said Sammy. "I found myself in real trouble several times along the way. I am thankful that you each taught me the tips and tricks to use when I'm down in those dark, chilly waters trying to *catch* the fish."

Suki Suick replied, "You worked hard and learned a lot, but if you think you found yourself in trouble, you have *no idea* of what *real trouble* looks like."

"Yes," croaked Francis Frog. "You've just moved into a box that is full of lures that have survived being in *real trouble*. That is why we call our home Tackle Box Troubles."

SS BETSY

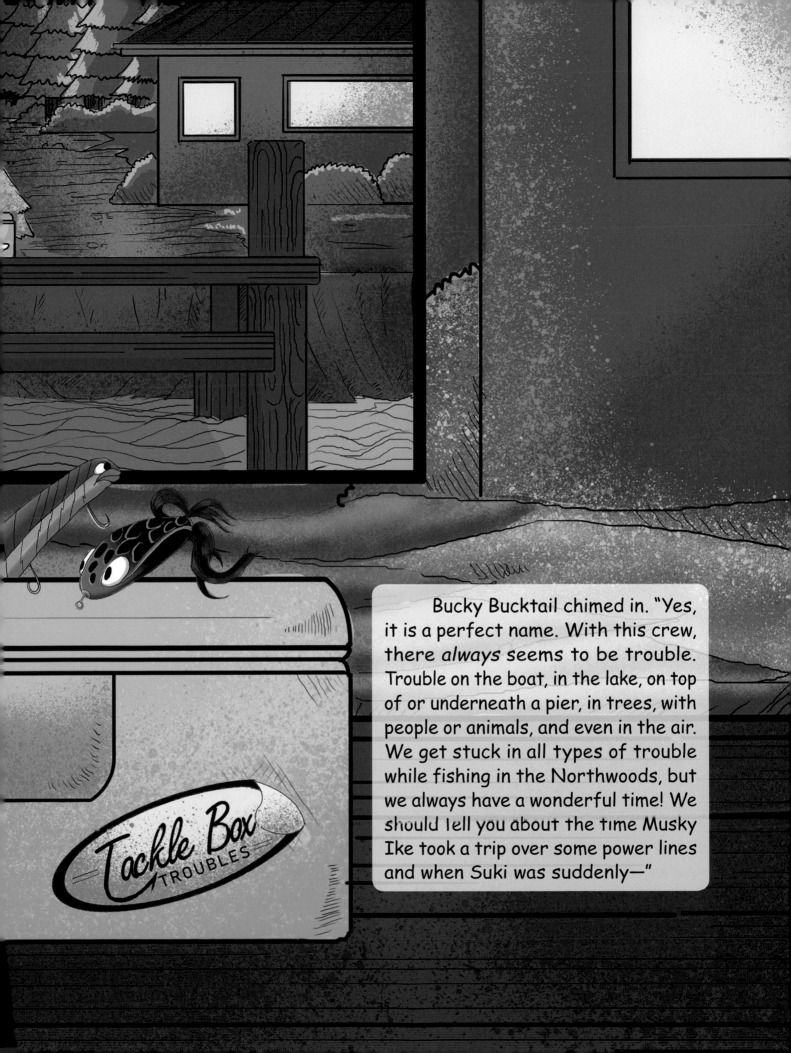

Bucky Bucktail chimed in. "Yes, it is a perfect name. With this crew, there *always* seems to be trouble. Trouble on the boat, in the lake, on top of or underneath a pier, in trees, with people or animals, and even in the air. We get stuck in all types of trouble while fishing in the Northwoods, but we always have a wonderful time! We should tell you about the time Musky Ike took a trip over some power lines and when Suki was suddenly—"

"Oooh, remember when Mr. Rodafeller was lost in the lake? We should tell Sammy that story!" croaked Francis, interrupting Bucky once again.

"Yes, I suppose we could share Mr. Rodafeller's story too. Although please remember, Francis, that Mr. Rodafeller is a fishing *rod*, not a fishing *lure*."

Francis thought about his story choice again, jumped up, and shouted excitedly, "Wait, Bucky! Sammy should hear *your* story first, because it involves a *dog!*"

Suki Suick turned to Sammy Spinner with a smile and said, "And sometimes the trouble is right here in this box."

As the fishing lures debated which story to share first, Sammy hung back by his hooks, knowing he would be happy to listen to all the trouble these lures had unhooked themselves from before he had arrived.

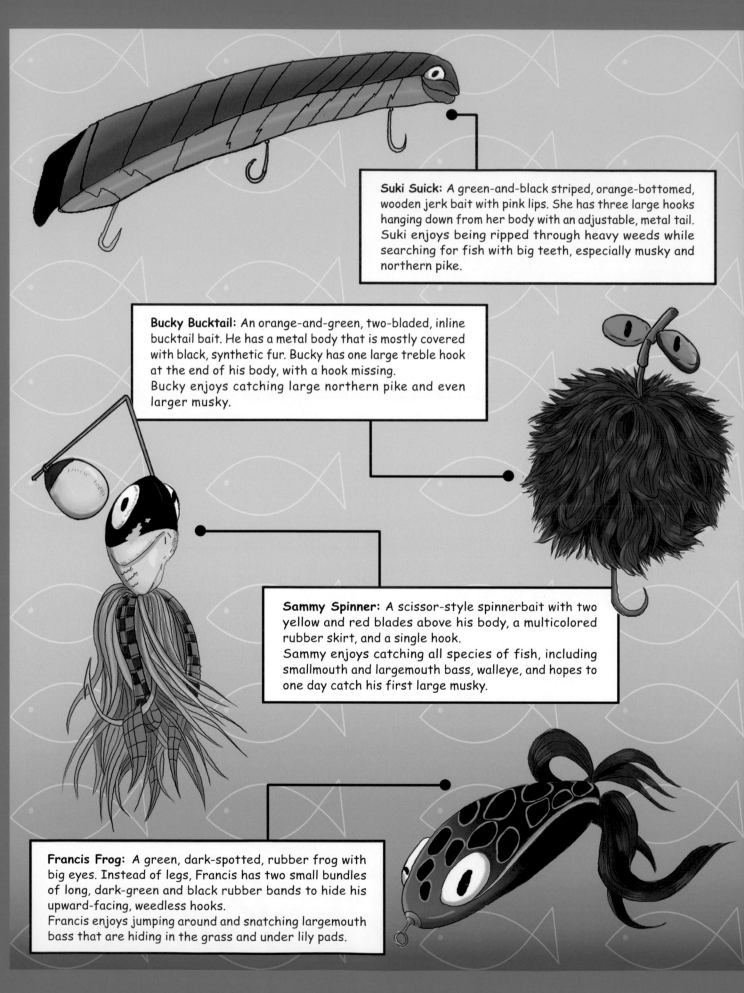

Suki Suick: A green-and-black striped, orange-bottomed, wooden jerk bait with pink lips. She has three large hooks hanging down from her body with an adjustable, metal tail. Suki enjoys being ripped through heavy weeds while searching for fish with big teeth, especially musky and northern pike.

Bucky Bucktail: An orange-and-green, two-bladed, inline bucktail bait. He has a metal body that is mostly covered with black, synthetic fur. Bucky has one large treble hook at the end of his body, with a hook missing.
Bucky enjoys catching large northern pike and even larger musky.

Sammy Spinner: A scissor-style spinnerbait with two yellow and red blades above his body, a multicolored rubber skirt, and a single hook.
Sammy enjoys catching all species of fish, including smallmouth and largemouth bass, walleye, and hopes to one day catch his first large musky.

Francis Frog: A green, dark-spotted, rubber frog with big eyes. Instead of legs, Francis has two small bundles of long, dark-green and black rubber bands to hide his upward-facing, weedless hooks.
Francis enjoys jumping around and snatching largemouth bass that are hiding in the grass and under lily pads.

Printed in the United States
by Baker & Taylor Publisher Services